TO INSIST THAT SOMETHING—SOMEONE
OR SOME BEING—CANNOT BE IMAGINED

IS, IN FACT, ITS OWN FORM OF
OPPRESSION

AHSAHTA PRESS

BOISE, IDAHO

2014

THE NEW SERIES

#65

AFTER-CAVE

MICHELLE DETORIE

Ahsahta Press, Boise State University, Boise, Idaho 83725-1525
ahsahtapress.org
Cover design by Quemadura / Book design by Janet Holmes

LIBRARY OF CONGRESS CATALOGING-IN-PUBLICATION DATA
Detorie, Michelle.
[Poems. Selections]
After-cave / Michelle Detorie.
pages cm.—(The New Series ; #65)
ISBN 978-1-934103-54-8 (pbk. : alk. paper)—ISBN 1-934103-54-3 (pbk. : alk. paper)
I. Title.
PS3604.E768A6 2014
811'.6--DC23
2014033565

ACKNOWLEDGMENTS

I am deeply and profoundly grateful to my family, friends, teachers, editors, and publishers for all their inspiration and support: Kurt Newman, Jessica Smith, Michalle Gould, Amy Boutell, C.J. Martin, Julia Drescher, Elka Karl, Randa Jarrar, Jenny Rowe, Amanda Ackerman, Harold Abramowitz, Mathew Timmons, Gillian Devereux, Ash Smith, Amish Trivedi, Matthew Henrickson, Susana Gardner, Juliana Leslie, Andrea Quaid, Andrew Porter, K. Lorraine Graham, Cole Cohen, Lauren Wilson, Nicole Detorie, Irene Skaff, Al and Ruby Newman, Patrick McKeever, Paula Smith, Beth Taylor-Schott, Jerry Pike, Tom Grimes, Kathleen Peirce, Cyrus Cassells, Andrew Hudgins, Karen Fish, James Hendrick, Elizabeth Treadwell, Bhanu Kapil, Janet Holmes, and my parents, Nick and Cindy Detorie. I love you all.

I would also like to thank the editors, publishers, and curators of venues where excerpts from *After-Cave* have appeared: *13 Myna Birds* ("The ruined house," "Lace is the sound," and "In the Tunnel"); *Coconut* ("six fingered window" and "all over again"); *Esque* ("under snow, the painted snow" [as "Assembly"] and *"OUT THERE*—gesturing with my one good arm" [as "The Results"]); *N/A* ("mesh water in the air," "I grow into a dog," "the animal women," "We just saw millionaires," and "There are four moons"); and Naropa's *Summer Writing Program Magazine* (excerpt from "FeralScape"). Poems from "Fur Birds" appeared in chapbooks for Insert Press and Dusie; poems from "FeralScape" appeared in a chapbook for Dusie. Selections from "Fur Birds" appeared in the *Collective Intelligence: Early Human Narratives* exhibit, March 2013, at the Interdisciplinary Humanity Center's Platform Gallery at the UC Santa Barbara. Selections from "Fur Birds" appeared in Handmade/Homemade Exhibit, March 2012, at Pace University.

CONTENTS

FUR BIRDS   1
FERALSCAPE   35
AFTER-CAVE   49

FOR THE GIRLS.

FOR THE CREATURES.

FOR EVERYBODY.

FUR BIRDS

I am 15. Female. Human (I think).

We lived in a burrow and ate grass. I licked my paw, tasting only the slightest remnants of ash. In one corner we piled sugar cubes—white and cold and sweet, and perfectly square. "Like a little igloo wall," my sister cooed, twitching her tail. The curtains were made of old bones and rattled when I looked outside.

In motion is how we live, sleeping inside skin. I want wheels turning only in, around. My clothes, they get thin as I get worn. We were looking out for tracing clouds, fin slid under wing. We were without beds. I nurtured sounds. We came to land on land like rest. We fluttered full to nest only sticks built into temporary chambers.

a squall of sour birds muffled by snow

gray light as you turn your eye the key

following the mean shadows
                men made
in doors, abandoned factories chiseled
in ruins as you pull wire from your ribs

the whole clockwork of forgiveness
impinged by the unfairness of it all—

you can barely swallow knowing
you've been so complicit, so cruel.

Sunday best was calico lace, glib feathers, underpinnings of sticks

             and river ribbons.

Clock marking the cinders.
   There was a procession
where profession to profession we crept, carrying branches.
Each of us was asked to speak, and it was with reluctance and kindness that I lied.

How queer the roots were! How wonderful! I was almost grateful for the anemic, rose-tinged buzz of the processing light, how it came down, mantis-like, through the curve of dirt. We breathed the shadows, dusty crusts of corsets and ribs. Magicked softly, I could detect the low, plump "wwwhhoooph" of the owls mounting one another in the glass dusk. We were so happy; the string we'd worked hard to harvest turned gold and breathing. Every crevice is an incidence of habitat. WE ARE SO GRATEFUL TO BE ALIVE.

It's beginning again: my impulse
to rake and weed. The moths
light up the lamb-wing. It's
dusk, and they don't trust
us. It's easy to see why not.

Every pebble makes a house.

Digging underground, I disrupted homes that did not belong to me
but wound deep and tethered together.
      I thought of coupling tunnels and the downward wind of tubed
          figure-eights.
        Like swans
              leaning in, their necks so long:
    the forged reflection
   the rubbed-out lake

the animal women
> come to life

in tiny houses, a town
> erupting among

roots. The bog breathes
> home into the bones

the grasses touch
> the air, the houses

their red jelly hearts
> settled in logs

of moss and rot
> beat through the clover.

I never thought of health, only of hunger. Hunger and eating
defined my definition of health. The heart beats blood through
filaments
flesh that feeds my house.

Dirt church where nothing dies.

I've forgotten all my songs. The garden
rows like swamped in ruins. Dust
in gates, mesh wire swinging. We'd
cling to ours if we'd only known.
She thought this to herself before bed
every night for a week.

two
dead things

when
did you become
so lonely?

one thing could
fit inside
the other: mouse, bird-
wing. glossy black
tail to feather

because I am
afraid of breaking
things

wick quick
to flame

everywhere
there is water
water

a body in the hand
(seed spread
through secret
channels)

every time
someone is kind
to me I feel
like breaking

It was about forgetting and hurt feelings & beginnings. We worked in rows, our arms swinging back and forth, the needle hemming slow and long, the stitch singing. When I closed my eyes she sings a song. She is my twin scissor. We swing and twitch the tune, the lungs brimming. At first it felt like all I ever wanted was a hug, and a lung. But now the burning coils of plastic unspool the glossed rots of synthetic hair and combs, watering cans, and crimson boots. All these others out there—out here—hand to hand we almost touch. No matter how we look at it—we are either all together or else we are all alone.

only half is visible

the way a mountain
and the ocean
look similar

blue, breaking

my face is
no face

what disappears
in the mirror there

my hand on wood—bureau, brush
handle, spoon

when you asked me
if the water was always so blue
your heart
beating
was your mouth
moving

the double-crested's singing happens
in gestures, backwards
zig-zagged shadow the flickering
script, amissed blinking

shutters on bone-flutters
a slough through, thickets
where the tubes entered
and carried you away

Automatic mirror, the slackening
of attention: what makes
      you pink. An eclipse
      loosened and turned
down a mountain, sym-
metrical delights in glass.

THE DATA IS FEMININE.

Your hand

like a little lock

reached through—

it opens with sticks.

Mesh-water in the air, the light
webs unmarshed. Waiting for June
to unlock. Creature-clocks.

    The acid lake winks
under ash, under motorized wings:
        eye snaps capture
        trees like glass, like little singed machines
        who haven't any hearts.

OUT THERE—gesturing
with my one good arm

the augurs scan
the horizon, how
it breaks through

black line to white line
the image weighted

opening my invisible skirts
fill the flue with tresses

millions to millions the cells scatter
too many ricochets to hold on

how long before it's too long
to come back

It's difficult to determine where to land. What's old to you is new to someone else. The body is broken into parts and yet flows together like water. I am animal; there is no becoming. I roam the various streams of information seeking the live bits—hoping something sticks. Words and songs and words and pictures moving and moving. The things you'll do because you love someone, because you're alive. If you're singing there is the hoping that someone is listening to the words. The words shake down yellow from the trees, gather-scatter over concrete. There's a fantasy of gathering them up in my arms, as if it were possible to hold them.

I come calling
      down to you
step slowly always
      as though the earth
      is composed of icy steps
and I'm reaching for
        the phantom railing.

    The slough gleams
    like fin-flashes
    out past the oil
        platforms, teeter-totter
            on the limb, horizon-
                      shed sun.

      Up here

    the clouds have
        legs.
      They crawl
      all over
            the mountains.

We measured the mountains.
This small sadness:
I can hold in my swale, taste
it on my tongue. Salt
showers and the glow
inside bones—lit up,
electric signs. The desert
is the pain of home, the home
away. This withholding—
it makes me pine all the more.
Sympathy is a craving. The stone
around us turns to ice.

Things you can do with bones:
collect them, arrange them
into houses—this way in
& this way out. Trade and measure.
Dig a moat. All the glitter
in the marrow nourishes
our divisions—gushing
mud, bridle-bearing ghosts
blown in from the neighboring
thickets. Tumbleweeds or
teeth? Imagine if you had
to choose. Fur
for a mouth—for
a moment. At night
all the mountains whisper-
echo the electric coral
reefs—choral, corral—
siphoned from the other
side of the word. Twin
vixens, we listen to mend
ends—to hasten—quicken.

PALM-PAWS, forget
who was here. Fox
scent on the air
but in the air, the trembling:
low hoot of the loon—
that hidden body.

we are skin, snow, unpacked
boxes opened like petals, skin

I towed a shovel, uncovered holes
and buried pears, I towed a line

and dragged it through a river
towards an ocean. I held

a line, a pail, my pockets
becoming full, the moon
blood red and lined with fur.

WE CARRY A RIFLE
     crooked all the way
     down, the mud ruts' roots
     grasping, skirts drug
     wrists red where
     there were furs.
               FUR BIRDS, the reeds
                   swinging, swished
                   hems under wings
                   exploded so quick
                   in our lungs it's like
                   the wings our hearts
                           exploded—

They say the war is over
as though saying a thing
makes it true, makes
it tick-tick time. A dome
within a dome: our
little world in our little
world—it's all ours!
The inside of our house
is the same as the outside:
it curves around and is
inside-out. The confidential
is relative: who knows who.
In the aisles we are all
wandering around as if
we are full
of little houses.
There's almost
no reason to go out.

A little angular house

on the edge of a hill

all swolled up,

all wedged still

below the deer, antler

hopes re-threading trees

re-threading homes

all about the wells –

the shimmer glimmer

tomes like a handbook

of mirrors, like running

when you're only filled

with the idea of running.

The windeye drifts

skullfars away: scatter-

yellow scales of light.

How young and bony-brave

we look standing all alone

in such a big, big wood.

Map matches twitching
in the glove, the wheel
gleaming. Shudder
shades, the trees
falling over your
face. Lash laces,
swum through
gaze uproad, upriver.

Your heart, it's a knot
of flames, a knave
of a feathers. In
the dream sea, green
words flex and shiver.

For hands, FUR BIRDS,
metal chains a-linking.
It's a messy sound—
gush and shatter.
Tongue to paw. Paw
to ground. Pause.
Pause. Repeat.

FERALSCAPE

Come in→

( )

I'm full of ruins

The omen of a
dark place becomes
strategic, liquid.

A small distance between
a book and a room.

A book is a room,
I am a house.

A house ~~whose~~ with fur

the pages clot with
the ruins of half-finished
places.

One is another whose fur
we pet in the dark
tunnel of a house.

thump, thump
in the dark narcotics

Little	House
Bloom	When
The	Sun
Comes	Up

                                                           back to the   House
                                                           by the time   When
                                                                   the   Sun
                                                                    is   Up

Little   rips out of the dark night.   Mirror feathers
Bloom   around the lips. An ear   for snow-blind
The   ses like worms writhing   Here she
Comes   wearing the lipstick of sm   udged sticks
                         smelling of   Possession

                A window   gives way
                 to gravel ,undergarments
                       the woods—the pines—
                                   yielded

Some birds
    dive
                                                                after
                                                                hunting

There are so many ways
            in which
                a girl and a bird
                    are similar   (we write about them
                                                              TOO MUCH)

                We write
      about them because they
                disappear

Sleep in levitation   Girls can levitate

                                                                 (but then we all forget)

The clouds more
        a type of organ
              with
      our pink

Some birds

      dive in the snow

          to sleep

There are so many pink bones
   in the yellow paper dress
     a girl wears into the woods. In this story the trees
     are sentences that blow away. \\\\\

                We become smokestacks, bewildered by the fur-lined limbs
             about them like buttressed electrics, coiled plastics
                  dismembering the air.

                                        your hand like a little lock reached through—
                                              it opens with sticks

sleep is like levitation
A telepathy of glass

South Carolina is
shaped like a heart:
like a fist

The clouds move
    a type of soft machinery
        with a wet self-consciousness
           hospitable to
our pink mold, our confection

                some ways
                   in which
            a page and a bird
               are similar

                we write
              them because
                  they
                  appear

     girls can levitate

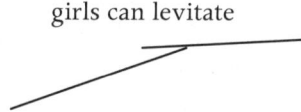

        We passed a zipper or chainsaw
    our notes through the organ
we sleekly become, without teeth
        or tongue like
      seam-ripped frocks:
silky, frayed, gleaming: a continuance

                    I let myself
                    soften after
                      hunting

a feralscape—a haunted place—of mud—of
"old filthy ruins"—nostalgia like a ghost
   lounging about—mucking things up.
     The mirror doesn't have an eye,
  it needs us to see it: to see it
                    we see ourselves.

       smell   of honey + meat
       taste   of burnt hair/fur
       touch   of hot, sinking asphalt—tar
       sound   of locusts, their chiseled drone of scissor-saws
       view   of a milk white morning
                  creeping

                back to a house

THE DATA IS FEMININE

AFTER-CAVE

Time is with the animal: It has a politics.

On a scale of 1 to 10, rate your level of pain.

I looked out the window and pretended

I was looking into your house.

It's obvious: the whole
world is haunted. Consider
the disasters and broken
spaces:

                    edge of a hole
      where a paw marks the edge
      of our map. A chart of stars
      for a fur-bird to make a course
      through blue, black—all the hues
            we love to lack.

                            Our lack is a fence
                            the same shade as ash.

The ruined house was where
we fell asleep. The old typewriter
with grass growing through thin
sunlight, starved of yellow
and almost white. Your hair
was yellow then, a spool
of floss wound with light.
& then the voices calling
us home. The shade got
cold. The dirt too, rich
and damp; in the right
light it sparkled.

Lace is the sound of the unwound
gun. See the deer tail bob through
leafless trees. I wonder if you miss
me the way I miss you. Remember
how the ferns made the snow
melt? The way they were warmer?
All summer I followed you who
followed the dog. It was natural
to follow animals, you said. Sometimes
in the woods I still look for you.

In the tunnel
we undid our lessons
asking for no things
but for those which could be made
from metal, plaster.

    I was afraid.
      Eclipse like paper
torn by clipped
sun. No pinion
but my glass jaw bobbing.
No owls in the catacombs.
Not a dry eye in the house.
No sudden for the wintered.

    Without the opened
    box we shaped our mouths
    like saucers
    and amid the floss left by antlers
    we sang to ourselves.
    I ask for nothing from you;
    you knaved, inventing feathers.

All over again, arrow thin
the air the medium form
forming soft as foam hands
clasped or else from skin skimming
over butter cloth. Do we win?
How does it end? Over as deer
clutter along fences flesh
and hair and black-tipped tails
feather, leafing out, scattering bells
pealed, pulled as if perfect came
as a pin cushion pursed for windows
and glassless winters chemicals.

We break up, become ourselves

In new arrangements

Of   sister, sister

Undersnow, the painted snow, the blood

and painted blood, black hooves

strike ice, strike lines perimeter

the glass factory. Inside

there's a makeshift church.

The fogged glass is stain-lit

under-snow fluorescence.

And bread unbreaking

black sky metal-cold

over the road no one

takes home. Huddled

together, paint chips

eclipse the real moon

or at least what's understood—

the sky we stood under.

Clean scissors, I beg
for rescue, for a pin
to tend the pain: pink
not newly, slit red
then blue. In purple
liquids I store
the pulse: thump
thump in the dark
narcotics. Fizz-
winged, my fissures
shore: approach
the winking beacon
of a still-life body:
smooth and porous, pried
free from every
pinching reign: stung
veins and stony ventricles.

                              the pipes closed a small slit

                                             fox scissors

for thinking darkly about the history

in the weather

                                   the mud bottom churned

in sinking promises, crafts

they unforgave and carried like frail

          assurances—paper cranes—in the bibs

                                             of our rivers

six-fingered window, double-joy, the jolt
that becomes the figured. ghost bones
on the pane, where wings spread, fast
appearing. the world's too rushed. I'm
against dying. slick in winter, iced fringes
of dead leaves in yellow. underfoot lines
getting wrinkled, text slinking into
a slurry of loose stems, betwixt
twinkling, the winking shone. sea
shivered in winter, pelican hovered
over oily rainbows, feathered letters
mixed with sticks littering the shore.

I let myself soften after hunting.

There are four moons and an ocean full of lead.

I thought of taking off my clothes and sleeping with the wolf. I wondered, would it be warmer? I struggled to see how the wolf and I could be different.

For now, my theory is that the trees have decided to grow underground, spreading toward the sparkle-grit of plasms they say we're floating on. Sticks become their own kind of treasure. We go out gathering.

the failure to occupy
breaks apart like soap
sand salt all
the things we need
to name

hook looking through
nothing to measure
such loneliness against
a net through—it isn't
there if we can't
spell it

[the underside/ when]

I do not know how to begin

the worm, or the heal

the ridged groove where your wing slid

[I am not open enough]

I want to open my mouth, but you—

—it's not a thing helped when wind
without a shell
hollows out your heart-bone, rib of when

there was a net;

see—on the horizon there—
a cleavage like a fin fluttering the shallow

eyes of pale yellow that do not blink

(It is evil, to imagine the self.

What would we dare to picture?

What would we dare to make?)

I grow into a dog. My paws are

soft numbers that print upon

the earth. The figures grow

into letters—text tracks

that spell a movement

from one shadow-self

into the next. A sort

of even-ing crescendo.

A sense is in the numbers—

a type of map: mud-body

of blood. and claws. and ash.

A fox came creeping along the horizon. By now, most of the trees were gone. Dried stalks of weather or crumpled piles of lumber. Somewhere, we thought, there must still be trees. It must be something in the water. But is it here? Can we see it?

The invisible air surrounds us as we sketch a dirt house. "Here is a kitchen. Here is a chair." We stumble 'round pretending to be full, to be drunk and happy. At least we have something to remember.

The babies, what will they know? Will it be easier to have not known the blue sky and the tacky quotidian contours of groceries and laundry? The luxury of having mail delivered—*right to the door of your house.* Red yarn wood of frequency. To-do lists. Turntables skipping.

When the planets turned, we began to slow down. The trains stopped running and the trucks stopped coming. We gathered in the grove of slippery elm and nursed the wolf cubs we recovered from the shallow graves excavated by the mother, the she wolf who hasn't returned, who we look out for.

When we see the fox, we are momentarily hopefully, but really we always knew the shadow shape moving was too small.

OUT HERE—

    something tricky happens to your sense of distance, your vision. Distance becomes its own sort of wall and everything cast shadows in it, no matter the position (or existence) of the sun.

We just saw millionaires in the gravel. They were still wearing watches. The last gleaming thing along the flesh. Their hands silver and dirty, turning to forks, clutches.

The mirage women bring us a pile of colorful presents, wrapped and ribboned and spilling out of hand wagon with three red wheels. We spend the afternoon unwrapping them, making the boxes into new houses, filling them with dirt, hoping that birds or worms or foxes would come to find them, us.

Tomorrow we will weave the bones of a cormorant into our dresses, and we will borrow the feathers. Nothing gets ruffled and everything is reused. Remember when there were birds? When there was color? Oh, that iridescent black glowing with green and purple: there was something written in it.

Today we tend to the tedious business of keeping house and rocking the fetal corpses to sleep, pretending birth can be re-visioned, revised and mended. We ourselves will go without sleeping, keeping vigil, lingering in the threshold of consciousness, waiting for the vision.

Black crust spills from the permeable lungs we created by stitching together the scraps of plastic we found among the schoolyard, the concrete mayhem chunked and powdered, but with bits of glitter and foam deep in the crevices where we can reach, we could read—or imagine at least—sorcery of weather, houses, water that runs on command.

I give birth
to a dog

I make room
in the river
and the wet

the blood and fur

It is over
so easily

———

we wanted scraps
were paper
to want to write

———

becoming
the moon comes down slow

———

creatures

a coalescing silence
memorized

———

what calls out
what carries

———

Pain is a window filling up with wings, a bent backwards bird saw
= curtains

tapered to neck-napes

it's a window full of birds
full of wings

everything else is smudged out
+

                                                you can't see through
                                                     the feathers

I struggle with the early darkness. You remind me that telling time is a gift, a system of repeating surfaces. I let my mind cling to this even though it feels wrong.

You tell me that the pyramids were the product of collaboration, innovative project management, but I know already that what made them was slave labor—a capsized river of bones and blood.

The details camouflage the crooks.

Their fat tears glitter like diamonds.

One day the task of counting was proposed. There was even talk of taking names, of making a list. Who would name themselves?

When I walk away from the group it feels like hell.

I tie the dogs to the ragged rope belt I wear around my waist. We go out wandering. Lately, I have become afraid that they will run away, disappear into the barrens and then not come calling back to me. I have this nightmare where the white dog disappears like smoke—turning gray and fading—against the trees that sway, sway in the moody, apocalyptic feelings gathered by the mountains, sad and eroding, darkening in the ashlight of dawn, or dusk. Whatever time of day it is, it doesn't matter. If a dog disappears like that, it's like nothing will ever happen again.

Time's to put away

until we forget

and open ourselves

accidentally; as if saying

"I learned from it" makes

a thing worth going through.

Furless, I wear a rack of bone like it's nothing, because it is—nothing—just a figment of air and light. That's all there is to bone, in this climate, a charade of the proper angles arranging themselves into an apparition of what was when, when we could spell, when we could remember—conjure.

To insist that something—someone or some being—cannot be imagined is, in fact, its own form of oppression.

I've tethered the dogs to a rope belt that I wear around my waist. We go out looking for sticks, for meadows still blue with the asphalt glitter that rained down from the other side of the continent. Who can continue for us in our absence? Who?

                                                  I hope it will be you.

ABOUT THE AUTHOR

MICHELLE DETORIE lives in Santa Barbara, California, where she edits Hex Presse and coordinates the Writing Center at Santa Barbara City College. She is the author of numerous chapbooks including *Fur Birds* (Insert Press), *How Hate Got Hand* (eohippus labs), and *Bellum Letters* (Dusie). In 2007, Michelle was awarded a National Endowment for the Arts literature fellowship, and in 2010 she won a direct-to-artist grant from the Santa Barbara Arts Collaborative for her public art project, The Poetry Booth. *After-Cave* is her first full-length collection.

AHSAHTA PRESS

SAWTOOTH POETRY PRIZE SERIES

2002: Aaron McCollough, *Welkin* (Brenda Hillman, judge)
2003: Graham Foust, *Leave the Room to Itself* (Joe Wenderoth, judge)
2004: Noah Eli Gordon, *The Area of Sound Called the Subtone* (Claudia Rankine, judge)
2005: Karla Kelsey, *Knowledge, Forms, The Aviary* (Carolyn Forché, judge)
2006: Paige Ackerson-Kiely, *In No One's Land* (D. A. Powell, judge)
2007: Rusty Morrison, *the true keeps calm biding its story* (Peter Gizzi, judge)
2008: Barbara Maloutas, *the whole Marie* (C. D. Wright, judge)
2009: Julie Carr, *100 Notes on Violence* (Rae Armantrout, judge)
2010: James Meetze, *Dayglo* (Terrance Hayes, judge)
2011: Karen Rigby, *Chinoiserie* (Paul Hoover, judge)
2012: T. Zachary Cotler, *Sonnets to the Humans* (Heather McHugh, judge)
2013: David Bartone, *Practice on Mountains* (Dan Beachy-Quick, judge)

AHSAHTA PRESS

NEW SERIES

1. Lance Phillips, *Corpus Socius*
2. Heather Sellers, *Drinking Girls and Their Dresses*
3. Lisa Fishman, *Dear, Read*
4. Peggy Hamilton, *Forbidden City*
5. Dan Beachy-Quick, *Spell*
6. Liz Waldner, *Saving the Appearances*
7. Charles O. Hartman, *Island*
8. Lance Phillips, *Cur aliquid vidi*
9. Sandra Miller, *oriflamme.*
10. Brigitte Byrd, *Fence Above the Sea*
11. Ethan Paquin, *The Violence*
12. Ed Allen, *67 Mixed Messages*
13. Brian Henry, *Quarantine*
14. Kate Greenstreet, *case sensitive*
15. Aaron McCollough, *Little Ease*
16. Susan Tichy, *Bone Pagoda*
17. Susan Briante, *Pioneers in the Study of Motion*
18. Lisa Fishman, *The Happiness Experiment*
19. Heidi Lynn Staples, *Dog Girl*
20. David Mutschlecner, *Sign*
21. Kristi Maxwell, *Realm Sixty-four*
22. G. E. Patterson, *To and From*
23. Chris Vitiello, *Irresponsibility*
24. Stephanie Strickland, *Zone : Zero*
25. Charles O. Hartman, *New and Selected Poems*
26. Kathleen Jesme, *The Plum-Stone Game*
27. Ben Doller, *FAQ:*
28. Carrie Olivia Adams, *Intervening Absence*
29. Rachel Loden, *Dick of the Dead*
30. Brigitte Byrd, *Song of a Living Room*
31. Kate Greenstreet, *The Last 4 Things*
32. Brenda Iijima, *If Not Metamorphic*
33. Sandra Doller, *Chora.*
34. Susan Tichy, *Gallowglass*
35. Lance Phillips, *These Indicium Tales*
36. Karla Kelsey, *Iteration Nets*
37. Brian Teare, *Pleasure*
38. Kirsten Kaschock, *A Beautiful Name for a Girl*
39. Susan Briante, *Utopia Minus*
40. Brian Henry, *Lessness*
41. Lisa Fishman, *FLOWER CART*
42. Aaron McCollough, *No Grave Can Hold My Body Down*
43. Kristi Maxwell, *Re-*
44. Andrew Grace, *Sancta*
45. Chris Vitiello, *Obedience*
46. Paige Ackerson-Kiely, *My Love Is a Dead Arctic Explorer*
47. David Mutschlecner, *Enigma and Light*
48. Joshua Corey and G.C. Waldrep, eds., *The Arcadia Project*
49. Dan Beachy-Quick and Matthew Goulish, *Work from Memory*
50. Elizabeth Robinson, *Counterpart*
51. Kate Greenstreet, *Young Tambling*
52. Ethan Paquin, *Cloud vs. Cloud*
53. Carrie Olivia Adams, *Forty-one Jane Does*
54. Noah Eli Gordon, *The Year of the Rooster*
55. Heidi Lynn Staples, *Noise Event*
56. Lucy Ives, *Orange Roses*
57. Peggy Hamilton, *Questions for Animals*
58. Stephanie Strickland, *Dragon Logic*
59. Rusty Morrison, *Beyond the Chainlink*
60. Tony Trigilio, ed., *Elise Cowen: Poems and Fragments*
61. Kathleeen Jesme, *Albedo*
62. Emily Abendroth, *]EXCLOSURES[*
63. TC Tolbert, *Gephyromania*
64. Cody-Rose Clevidence, *Beast Feast*
65. Michelle Detorie, *After-Cave*

This book is set in Apollo MT type
with Helvetica Neue Extended titles
by Ahsahta Press at Boise State University.
Cover design by Quemadura.
Book design by Janet Holmes.

AHSAHTA PRESS
2014

JANET HOLMES, DIRECTOR
ADRIAN KIEN, ASSISTANT DIRECTOR

DENISE BICKFORD
KATIE FULLER
LAURA ROGHAAR
ELIZABETH SMITH
KERRI WEBSTER